Worship the Countryside

—some comments on the worship aspects of the report of the Archbishops' Commission on Rural Areas

by
David Cutts
Rector of Coddenham with Gosbeck and Hemingstone with Henley
Diocese of St. Edmundsbury and Ipswich

GROVE BOOKS LIMITED
Bramcote   Nottingham   NG9 3DS

CONTENTS

ACKNOWLEDGEMENT

Quotations from *Faith in the Countryside* are reproduced by kind permission of the Archbishops' Commission on Rural Areas.

THE COVER PICTURE

is by Peter Ashton

First Impression October 1990

ISSN 0305-3067
ISBN 1 85174 160 7

1. INTRODUCTION

The report of the Archbishops' Commission on Rural Areas (subsequently referred to as 'the report' in this booklet) was published on 11 September 1990. Entitled *Faith in the Countryside*[1] it addresses a wide range of topics. In essence it imitates its predecessor *Faith in the City*, the report of a similar commission reporting on the urban areas of this country. It therefore contains a mixture of recommendations, some of which are addressed to the government and some to the church in its various guises.

The main text of the report is just over 300 pages long with several appendices bringing the number of pages to nearly 400. It is pleasantly laid out and seems to be very readable, bearing in mind what it is actually meant to be. Out of the many recommendations[2] 47 are considered to be principal ones and these are very varied in content. For example number 6 in the list of these main recommendations[3] is about the funding of Training and Enterprise Councils whereas number 19 in the list is more general, being about the need for the church to be more outward-looking.

There was a great deal of concern that the report (like its predecessor) would be leaked to the press in advance of publication. In the end, despite the careful planning, a report did appear in a Sunday newspaper just before publication which had the effect of focussing attention on the recommendations directed at the government rather than the report in general. This is a pity, because the report is very good in many ways and has certainly been worth the wait. Great things were expected of the report by many people ministering in rural areas. Inevitably some of those hopes have not been fulfilled because a report of this length cannot hope to cover all the ground.

This present booklet is an attempt to demonstrate precisely this point with regard to the parts of the report which are to do with worship. The next chapter will attempt to set the scene before listing some of the pre-publication hopes of what the report might cover. The main section will then look in detail at the relevant chapter of the report, measuring it against these expressed hopes.

In the end the author's aim (and that of the Group for Renewal of Worship in commissioning the booklet) is to generate discussion. We understand that the Archbishops' Commission have that aim firmly in view as well and are therefore welcoming this sort of material.

---

[1] Published by Churchman Publishing Limited in paperback at a cost of £12.50. It should be readily available from bookshops.
[2] I haven't had a chance to add up the total!
[3] Listed on pages 313ff.

2. THE COUNTRYSIDE TODAY

The title that I have given to this chapter might suggest that somehow there is one view of the countryside which all will recognize. This is, of course, entirely false! To demonstrate this, here are various ways of looking at a small part of the countryside:

Firstly the scene before our eyes looks like something straight out of a John Constable painting. There is a green pleasant landscape with gentle hills rolling down towards a picturesque cottage built of stone. The cottage is obviously inhabited because we can just about discern the wispy spiral of smoke from the chimney. Nearer to us there are sheep grazing on the side of the hill. Beyond the cottage there are signs of a growing crop. It has rained earlier but now the sun is breaking through the clouds. Everything looks fresh and new and delightful.

The second picture is of the same scene in February. Now the grass is covered by several inches of snow. The picture is very different but to an onlooker just as delightful. Particularly attractive are the droplets of snow hanging on the branches of the trees. The scene would make a good Christmas card picture. No-one points out that the old lady who lives in the cottage is running out of fuel for her fire. The snow has made the roads impassable so her daughter who lives in a nearby town cannot reach her. The old lady declines to have the telephone installed in her rented cottage. The landlord declines to provide an inside toilet or a bathroom.

The third picture is of the same scene in August. It is nearly midnight and the old lady cannnot sleep because they are harvesting the crop in the field behind her cottage. It isn't just the noise of the combine harvester but its floodlights keep her awake as well, as they periodically sweep across her bedroom wall. She daren't complain to the farmer—he is her landlord as well. Besides she knows they have to work all hours nowadays. It is very different from when her husband was alive and working on the farm.

The fourth picture is of the same scene several years later. The farmer has had several poor harvests and was forced to sell the cottage to raise some much-needed capital. He got a good price for it because of its secluded location. The old lady has gone to live in the same town as her daughter. She is glad to be near her family but hates the noise of the town. She had lived in the cottage all her life. Now it is all different. Someone who is away in London during the week lives there at weekends. He has installed a bathroom and is hoping to build on an extension for another bedroom. He is taking legal advice about the farmer working at night in the fields around his cottage.

The report stresses that the countryside is changing and rapidly so. The rural idyll no longer exists. It probably never did for most of the people who lived there. The life of a farm labourer in the past was particularly hard.

Many of these changes are because the personnel involved are different. The days of 'the rich man in his castle, the poor man at his gate'[1] are over,

---

[1] A verse from the original version of 'All things bright and beautiful', now omitted from most hymn books but still to be found in the unrevised version of *Ancient and Modern* and therefore sung, I suspect, in many village churches, including two of my own.

and now all kinds of people can be found living in villages. One way of looking at this is to imagine that the village inhabitants can be split into several groups[1] , namely the farmers, the old villagers, the new villagers and the retired. The people in each of these groups have very different expectations of village life.

The farmer sees the village as a place of work and little else. The days of labour-intensive farming have long since departed and now it could be described as a highly technological industry. Many farmers would believe that the land is theirs to do what they like with it. This is not to say that their use of it is necessarily irresponsible, but rather that they believe that what goes on is little to do with anyone else. In fact many farmers try very hard to act in what they believe is a very caring way in their usage of the land. They wish more people would realize that and they get frustrated by the way everyone seems to have an opinion about the use of the countryside. They have little use for village facilities and don't attend parish functions because people avoid speaking to them. Their children will probably marry other farmers' children and they will build new houses on the farm for them all, if they are allowed to, thus creating a little world of their own.

The 'old villagers' are those who have lived in their respective villages most, if not all, of their lives. If they are 'immigrants' then they will not have moved far, and the move will have been due to marriage or a change in work circumstances. They differ from the farmers (who may also have lived locally all their lives) in that the farmers are and certainly were the employers. The 'old villagers' were (now rarely are) those who were employed locally, either in farming, or perhaps in one of the many related industries. They see the village as a place to live, possibly as a place to work, and as a place to relax after work. They will want to patronize the village shops (if there are any), and the village pub, and will want to go to events of their choosing in the village hall. They may be reliant on local buses and also on the sub-post office for pensions and allowances. Their children would have liked to stay in the village when they married but had to move away because the cost of housing was more than they could afford.

The 'new villagers' are those who have chosen to move to the village, probably in a search for somewhere quiet to live where they can bring up their family, safe from the pressures of urban life. They may stay in the village for many years ('many' being a relative word and in this case meaning over 10), but are perhaps more likely to move away as promotion at work means moving to head-office or whatever. They see the village primarily as a place to relax away from work. The wives have their own transport and can drive the children to school, cubs, and ballet lessons and themselves to evening classes, all of which take place elsewhere. They frequently complain at parish meetings of the way that 'all this traffic' is destroying the village. They are of course thinking of everyone else's cars. They never shop in the village because it is cheaper and far more convenient to use the nearest supermarket. They have been inside the village

[1] This is obviously simplistic but still conveys some important points.

pub but prefer to go to a real country pub with a proper rustic atmosphere. The village hall was useful when the children were younger because a mothers and toddlers group met there. Now they only go there for the annual parish meeting. They will have left the area by the time their children come to get married.

The retired people in the village are obviously a mixture of all the previous three groups, though farmers often do not usually retire in the conventional sense.[1] Particularly noticeable are those who have chosen to retire to a village after living all their working lives in towns. In many ways they are like the 'new villagers' but often, certainly at first, they are very lonely, because they are trying to come to terms with retirement as well as moving to a new area. They see the village then as somewhere for them to be active but relaxed (these two desires are not as contradictory as they at first sound). The village hall may be the scene of their activity or perhaps the local church. They may want to get onto the parish council or form a community council. They will in fact do a lot which seems on the face of it to be very helpful. They cannot understand why others do not always share their enthusiasm.

These descriptions are obviously caricatures and therefore grossly unfair. Having said that, the author recognizes something of himself in the description of the 'new villagers'.[2] Similarly readers who live in rural areas may see themselves as well as being in one of the groups (or may perhaps prefer to make their own categories).

As well as being a caricature it is also a sweeping generalization which does not fit many parts of this country.[3] The analysis may then be invalid but it does illustrate something very important.

The main point of this chapter so far has been to stress not only the changing nature of the countryside but also that there are many tensions and problems contained there and often hidden from a visitor's view. The myth of the rural idyll is then perpetuated both by these same visitors but also by those who live in the village and would prefer to keep the tensions firmly hidden.[4]

It is in this environment that the country church is placed and seeks to worship and minister. The ACORA report underlines the need for the rural church to think of the context in which it exists.[5] It affects every aspect of church life and certainly the worship. It is therefore against this background that the rest of this booklet is written.

[1] Neither do clergy!
[2] Clergy are almost invariably 'new villagers' by nature of their work, which actually raises all sorts of interesting questions about rural ministry. However these questions are strictly beyond the scope of this booklet.
[3] Such as mining areas for example.
[4] Several years ago I upset a parishioner by mentioning in a sermon that some villagers had no inside washing or toilet facilities. She admitted to me that she did not mind a discussion of such basic matters from the pulpit but rather that she would prefer her idea of the countryside to remain unchanged. She has now gone to live in a town.
[5] See in particular the opening pages of chapter 8.

3. ISSUES CONCERNING WORSHIP

During the period leading up to the publication of the ACORA report, with the help of the Group for Renewal of Worship, I compiled a list of issues which are particular to the church in the countryside. This list, which is described below in the form of a series of questions, is hardly exhaustive but is culled from various sources including members of the Group who live and minister in the coutryside. There is no significance in the order of the headings nor of the order of the questions within those headings.

1. The leading of worship
Now that the days of one resident clergyman per parish are definitely over, who is to lead the worship in the local church? Should it fall to the incumbent who may live several miles away and who may have several services to take every Sunday morning? Should it be 'left' (very loaded word) to the laity and, if so, who and how many of them and who will train them? Will these same lay people have sufficient time to prepare for their task, bearing in mind their other commitments? Are there any theological principles as to who is the right person to lead the worship in a given community?

2. The type of services
Assuming that it is impossible to provide Mattins, Holy Communion and Evensong in a village church every Sunday, which services are preferable? Should it be the same every week? What is the theological issue here about frequency of communion? Where do so-called 'family services' fit in? Should a mixture of the Book of Common Prayer and the Alternative Service Book be used or is there a theological principle involved? What is the place of recent liturgical publications such as *Patterns for Worship?*[1] How can all those who wish to worship be accommodated, bearing in mind the range of people likely to be present and the need to satisfy both charismatics and members of the Prayer Book Society?

3. The times of services
Should services be at the same time every week in the same church? Is this feasible? How does the frequency of eucharistic worship affect this?

4. The frequency of attendance
Is there a different expectation in the countryside from the town (i.e. less often in the countryside)? Should those in leadership be expected to go weekly?[2]

5. The particular problems of small congregations
Is there any answer to the discouraging experience of being in a nearly empty church where the singing is feeble? What are the special difficulties of preaching to only a few people?

6. Music
Is the organ the best instrument for a country church bearing in mind the difficulty of finding an adequate organist and also that feeble singing is no

---

[1] Published by the General Synod in 1989.
[2] This question may startle some readers, but in a church not far from here the PCC has a membership of 16 but the average congregation is 3.

match for strident organ playing?[1] What other alternatives are readily and realistically available? What sort of music should be used? Is chanting helpful? Are choirs and/or music groups feasible, bearing in mind that a small choir may do more harm than good?

7. Resistance to change

Is this accentuated in the countryside? What are the roots of it? What can be done to combat it? Should it be combatted at all?

8. Folk religion

Is this title fair to use in the countryside to describe the apparently tenuous links that people have with their local church and are only revealed at times such as baptisms? Is there a greater expectancy amongst country people of the role of the church? What place today have harvest services, Remembrance Sunday, Rogation Sunday etc? Is there a particular rural spirituality? Do funerals differ significantly from those in an urban setting? Is the rural church a gathered community 'called out' of the world?

9. Ecumenical

What if the Church of England is the only denomination with a church building in the village? What place do joint activities have, especially when the Church of England may dominate numerically? Are Local Ecumenical Projects feasible? Is there still a division between church and chapel?

10. Multi-parish groups

Is there a place for regular benefice services, bearing in mind that often the only common ground a group of villages has is the clergyman they share? How does this relate to any theological understanding of the church meeting within the community which it serves? What effect do episcopal services such as institutions, confirmations etc have on any such understanding?

11. The role of the deanery

Is there a place for a wider celebration? How can the weekly worship of the local church relate to this?

12. Children and young people

How can the needs of children be realized in worship in the countryside? Where and when should Sunday schools meet, bearing in mind the restricted facilities in some villages? What difference does it make to have two children present in a congregation of eight?

13. Religious communities

Is there a place for such groups in the countryside today? How can they help the local church and its worship?

14. Church organizations

How do they affect worship, especially groups such as the bellringers?

15. Buildings

How can a congregation cope with a building which is both an asset and a liability? What about the re-ordering of church buildings? Does it make a difference that the building is set in a churchyard which is still in use? Is a medieval building the best place for a small Christian community to meet for worship?

---

[1] The question may be as to whether an organ is the right instrument for any church but perhaps we have to make some assumptions.

4. ANSWERS THE REPORT OFFERS

Chapter 2 of the ACORA report is entitled 'Theological Reflections'. This is an interesting and well-written chapter with a good discussion of the place of people in the created order. What is noticeable however is that there is very little there about worship and the need we have as humans to relate to our God in this way. The lack occurs again when in chapter 8 there is some discussion about the role of the church.[1]

This discrepancy is very regrettable because there seems to be a lack of theological thinking which could and should have undergirded the whole of the chapter on worship. On the other hand there has been a very real attempt to address some of the issues which occur in the rural church, and it is interesting to note that nearly all of the headings of the previous chapter in the Booklet prove in fact to relate to topics covered in the relevant chapter of the report.

This chapter is number 9, and has been called 'Spirituality and Worship'. The members of the Commission are to be applauded for linking these two matters together because they are strictly inseparable, particularly in the rural church where spirituality is often hard to determine precisely.[2] On the other hand the chapter is very unbalanced in its content. For example section 9.42 raises the very practical point of the needs of the hard of hearing, but fails to really get to grips with the major issue here of whether the Christian community should be meeting in a building which presents so many practical difficulties.

For the rest of this chapter the report will be considered by comparing the material presented with the issues listed in the previous chapter of this booklet. The figures in brackets refer to the relevant section of the report.

1. The leading of worship
In the chapter of the report concerning ministry, the Commission describes the role of the parish priest as follows (8.19):

1. To be aware of the full breadth of the mission of the Church in its priestly, pastoral and prophetic aspects.
2. To share in this vision with the corporate body of the people of God in the parish, coming together in worship.
3. To focus with others on what can and should be done in ministry, using the gifts of all members of the body.

This is a helpful description and provides a useful 'launching-pad' for what the report says about the leadership of worship. The following paragraph immediately highlights the problem by talking about priests needing to avoid any thought of doing all this by themselves.

This is very noticeable in worship in multi-parish groups. It is almost physically impossible for the minister to lead every act of worship in such

---

[1] In particular see section 8.6.
[2] In my experience country people, including 'immigrants', find it harder to articulate what they actually believe, compared with their urban cousins.

a group and the report gives a good description of the problems of trying to do this (9.24). Thus for very practical reasons there is a need to involve lay people in the leading of worship.

It does of course go further than this and there is an important principle at stake. At the press conference at which the report was launched the Bishop of Norwich said that in his experience the 'live' churches were those where the laity were involved in the leadership of worship. Many town churches discovered this a while ago—and presumably came to that decision to involve others for theological reasons to do with the nature of the church, rather than for mere pragmatic reasons to do with the local priest not being able to arrive until after the service was due to start.

This then leads on to deciding who should be the people to lead the worship. The report is most refreshing when it avoids the trap of assuming that only accredited lay ministers such as readers can do this. Just as there is always the danger of the priest doing everything, there is also the problem of simply creating another level of 'special people' who yet again inhibit genuine sharing in ministry. This can be a very controversial issue in parishes, particularly where readers (or others with some form of bishop's commission) have, in the past, had a monopoly of standing in for the priest. The report handles this with great sensitivity in its chapter on ministry (8.88ff).

Instead of placing any restraints on who should lead worship the report seeks to give broad guidelines (9.31ff). It stresses the need to find people who have some standing in the local community (which may not be the people who think they have that position!) whilst also reminding us that there are already people available such as mentioned in the last paragraph and also the churchwardens (8.86).[1]

The report also encourages the involvement of as many people as possible in the planning of worship through the use of worship groups etc (9.12 and 9.32). Many parishes have found this to be liberating experience, not least in that those who have been involved in planning an act of worship may feel more ready to help lead it. The only danger can be if such a worship group becomes too static and becomes in turn a power-base in the parish with a strong power of veto. One way of avoiding this is to have a group which meets for a few months before the membership changes to let others take a turn.

The report also prints part of the Bishop of Norwich's visionary plan for his diocese (9.36). This describes a very different church from that which people are used to, but it is something which will have to come if the rural church is to survive. The Bishop mentions the priest coming to celebrate Holy Communion with the people and this of course raises the whole question of the frequency of eucharistic worship, mentioned again below. The report does offer the solution of lay people administering previously consecrated bread and wine ('extended communion') but does not discuss a central issue here.

[1] There may be a dichotomy here between the elected office bearers in the parish and those whose style is more 'charismatic'. The report does not really explore this.

What is lacking here is some thoughts on the nature of the leadership of the local church and the relationship of such leadership to the conduct of worship. There is some logic in seeing the people (i.e. the laity) who actually live in the village to be the leaders of the church rather than some clergyman who lives several miles away. If these people are truly the leaders of the local church, then should they not preside at its major functions? Therefore section 9.29 is not correct in seeing the only fundamental objection to extended communion in being the nature of the bread and wine. There is another basic problem in thinking about the nature of presidency.

2. The type of services

The report only briefly discusses this issue of frequency of communion services (9.26) and again fails to address a central issue. It almost implies that it is selfish of congregations to want regular eucharistic worship, not because of the demands this might place on the ordained ministry, but because of the apparent exclusion of many of those who would like to worship. This may leave us wondering what happened to the concept of the Lord's service for the Lord's people on the Lord's day. Undoubtedly some will feel excluded but this does not automatically imply that one should not have the service so frequently. Instead it raises questions of who should be admitted to communion (and particularly with regard to children and other unconfirmed but believing people) and also far more fundamental questions about what is appropriate worship for a Christian community. It says something about the way that this feeling of being left out can lead to an interest in confirmation, and this in turn can lead to a profession of faith.

Reflection on these issues may lead to the same conclusion that the frequency of communion needs to be carefully examined. The hard work needs to be done first, rather than trying to see it entirely in terms of its effect on non-communicants.[1]

Later on (9.43f) the report raises the issue of whether the Book of Common Prayer or the Alternative Service Book should be used, pointing out that some parishes have found Rite B to be common ground. The report calls this a fundamental matter (and it is) but does not address the fundamental question, namely the theological issue of whether it is more appropriate to address God in the language of the seventeenth century or to attempt to use more contemporary language.[2] A cynic might say that Rite B is only called 'common ground' because it is neither one thing nor the other, lacking the 'beauty' of the Prayer Book and the relevance of Rite A.

The Commission takes this further by mentioning their concern that younger clergy are not familiar with the Prayer Book. The report does not say what should be done about this. Are theological colleges meant to have some sort of token use of the Prayer Book (which must therefore be

---

[1] In my (no doubt limited) experience, a more important matter is *how* such worship is conducted rather than whether or not the service on offer is a Parish Communion.

[2] The word 'attempt' is deliberate, because it could be argued that the phrases of the Alternative Service Book hardly have an everyday ring about them.

totally artificial)? In the end surely the issue is whether the church is preparing its ordinands for the church of tomorrow or the church of today and, if it is the latter, *which* church of today?[1]

The report has some positive and helpful things to say about family worship (9.46ff). It is to be hoped that publication of the report will encourage the production of some good resource material for rural churches which takes into consideration the small numbers often involved.

3. The times of services

In the chapter on ministry the report identifies as a major problem the difficulty of meeting the expectations of those who are used to one clergyman to one church (8.70). This pressure can come from two groups of people, both from the elderly villagers who can recall when the church in their village had its own parson, and also from the incomers whose church experience has been that of urban parishes.

Sometimes this problem is focused on the difficulty of fixing the times of services. If a clergyman has several villages under his care and there are conflicting demands for his time on Sunday mornings it will probably prove impossible for any one church to have all its services at the same time each week. This again is contrary to the expectations of those who are used to going to church at the same time each week.

Before the ACORA report was published a rumour was being spread that the Commission were going to recommend that, come what may, each church should meet every week at the same time. Fortunately they have avoided doing this. It is perhaps an ideal to work towards, particularly where the local church assumes a greater responsibility for leading its own worship. However in the present climate this is difficult to achieve, and, if pushed, can mean that a more dominant church in a benefice will barge all the others into touch, by hogging the main morning slot and expecting the clergyman to take their services.

In the end what is required is a sensible arrangement worked out at benefice level, perhaps by the churchwardens meeting with the incumbent. It may still prove possible for each church to have their own particular time for several Sundays a month with careful planning and some genuine understanding of each others' needs. Coupled with this there needs to be a willingness not to expect too much of the ordained man. The report recommends (9.24) that a 'clergyman should only take two main morning services each Sunday'. This seems perfectly reasonable but even then he is likely to be under severe time pressure if we bear in mind that the first of the services can hardly start much earlier than 9.45, if families are to be welcomed, and the second not much later than 11.00, if people

---

[1] This booklet isn't of course written in a vacuum and the author is influenced by his own experience. Despite being a 'younger' clergyman (certainly by rural standards) he has considerable experience of Prayer Book services, both in former years as a layman and since ordination (though not much at theological college!). Over half the services in the monthly pattern of this group of parishes use the Prayer Book and it has to be said that the attendance at the modern language services far outsrips the number of people to be found at the services using traditional language.

are to have their lunch at a reasonable time. In between the services he will be expected to socialize with the first congregation before driving several miles to the next church and trying to arrive in good time.

4. The frequency of attendance
The report only covers this issue by implication whilst talking about family services (9.46). Here the assumption is that such services will be on a monthly basis and therefore the expectation seems to be that many of the worshippers will only come infrequently. This may be so in many places,[1] but there is a serious problem here. If people are only being encouraged to worship once a month, what happens if they are unavoidably not able to be present on a couple of those Sundays? Surely the aim should be to accept that some, perhaps many, will only come occasionally, but we should at least try to have something acceptable on offer more frequently?

This though presents a difficulty of its own. If 'family worship' happens fortnightly then there is a risk of splitting into two groups those who might come, rather than them coming twice a month. Then the sense of the whole of the church family at worship loses its driving force.

There is no easy answer to this and each church needs realistically to assess its own worship pattern. One possible way forward is to have a regular monthly family service but to intersperse such services with various special worship events, so that in reality more frequent family worship is on offer. It may then prove possible to encourage people to come to church more than once a month.

This is not, of course, only an issue for family worship. If a rural church has a different type of service each week then it may be that people will only come to the sort of service they like, which may only occur once a month. Hence a group who, for example, will only attend Prayer Book Mattins grows up and so on. A possible solution here may be the way that the services are planned right across the multi-parish group. If a particular type of service is available somewhere most Sundays, then it is at least *possible* that peoples' reservations about travelling to another church may be overcome by their desire to attend a service which they particularly like.

All this may sound highly undesirable, particularly to people who have little experience of the rural church. But no situation is ideal and this sort of compromise may be all that is possible. Most urban churches have a group who will only attend an early morning communion. This is a parallel problem but harder to solve satisfactorily.

5. The particular problems of small congregations
The report allocates several pages to the question of clergy training (8.27ff) and highlights the unsuitability of much of such training for rural ministry. Elsewhere (9.16 and 9.38ff) it talks of the discouragement felt by some rural clergy and recognizes that this is partly to do with the difficulties of leading worship for only a few people each week.

[1] It certainly is in my parishes and others known to me.

For those with no experience of this it is almost impossible to put into words the depression that this can cause for some clergy. Many clergy come originally from large, 'successful', suburban churches where (so it is alleged) hundreds gather each week to hear long erudite sermons which are part of well organized acts of worship where the singing is hearty and the soul is readily uplifted.

In contrast to this, leading less than ten people in worship, week after week, in cold rural churches with poor singing can be very dispiriting for the leader (and probably for the congregation). There is also a psychological problem to overcome when one thinks whether it is worth preparing a sermon for so few people.

The report is absolutely right when it stresses that a small church is not a failed large one (9.38). It is possible to make sense of such worship and the report encourages its readers to be realistic about this. It makes a few practical suggestions but there is much more that needs to be said here. Perhaps as above[1] the report will generate some enthusiasm for people to produce some suitable resource books.[2]

6. Music
In this area the report (9.59ff) is absolutely practical and realistic and there is little that can be added. Particularly helpful is the way that the myth that an organ is essential is attacked; and the readiness to suggest other forms of music will encourage those working in this field.

7. Resistance to change
On page 193 of the report there is a short list of 'things to be avoided' in worship in a rural church. The last thing on list, produced by 'an experienced country clergyman' is intriguing. Apparently new forms of service should only be used when they have been properly introduced. This author may be being unduly cynical but he feels that this is another way of saying never.

One of the difficulties experienced by many clergy in rural church life is resistance to change. It is particularly hard to cope with this when those who shout loudly against any change are those who have embraced modern ideas in every other part of their lives. Such resistance to change is not just to do with age. Often the older people in a village will welcome modern services or music if they can see why such things are being introduced. It may be the newcomer to the village who wants to maintain a village myth and will resist the introduction of *Mission Praise*[3] or whatever.

[1] See page 12 above for a similar comment.
[2] I have written further on this topic in Grove Worship booklet 108 *Worship in Small Congregations*, a title which the report mentions on page 195. However this really is only scratching the surface and there must be people with far more experience in this field who can share such knowledge in print.
[3] The report notes on page 201 the popularity of this hymn book and the author would echo such findings. It is genuinely 'ancient and modern' and for that reason (and because it is very cheap!) people welcome it.

My objection to the phrase on page 193 is the use of the words 'properly introduced'. There are two problems here. One is that what one person might reckon is sufficient introduction is very different from the expectation of another, especially if the latter person is determined to oppose any change. In this case the introduction may *never* be proper enough and the phrase 'not properly introduced' could provide a rallying cry for those opposed to change. The second thing is that part of any genuine introduction to anything new is actually the sampling. Is there really no room for experiment?

The report rightly advises caution and sensitivity (9.13) when handling conflict between groups in the church. However it is too simplistic to identify new ideas with incomers in opposition to the locals. The existing residents may long for change, especially if it will mean more people coming to the church of which they are very proud and have struggled to keep going over the years.

8. Folk religion

This is a terrible title to this section and I hope that I have not annoyed too many people by using it. However it serves as a sort of shorthand to describe the very tenuous but real links that many people have with their local church. The report avoids the title and instead talks positively about 'implicit religion' (9.1ff). This is a very important matter and it is a pity that the report did not devote more space to it.

On the face of it, it does seem that country people (including those who have moved out from the town) have a greater expectation of the church than those who live in urban areas. There are two ways of meeting this expectation and they are virtually diametrically opposite. The first way is for the church to see itself entirely as a gathered community living up to its name as those 'called out' from the community. In this case those 'outside' will be seen to be precisely that and will need to be directly evangelized to draw them in.

The second possibility to see the church in much vaguer terms with indefinite boundaries which embrace all those who believe they have a part to play in church life, however infrequently they attend worship. Evangelism then is more to do with drawing people closer to Christ rather than expecting them to cross any particular boundary. A further complication is that many of those involved in this way may find it impossible to articulate what it is that they actually believe.

Put starkly, the problem is that the former appears to be the New Testament model for the church whereas the second is the rural reality. It is important for a church to know which model it is using because it has great implications for every part of its life including its worship.

One of the occasions when this is most noticeable is at funerals. The report rightly identifies these to be major village occasions (9.57) and there will be an expectation that the church is the only appropriate place for the farewell to the person who may not have been there much during his or her life. Such desire to hold the funeral in church can be much misunderstood by those at church who cannot hold with the rather diffuse understanding of what the church is. They then feel that the family is 'using' the church, whereas, from the 'diffuse' point of view, the family are expressing the 'implicit religion' mentioned in the report.

There are no easy answers to this. The greatest danger is the implanting of an urban understanding of the church onto the rural setting. This is hard to avoid, if we bear in mind that the seed bed for many church leaders is the urban church. The implications for worship are manifold and the report takes a positive line (9.51ff), seeing the special occasions as times for celebration. This is right, but the danger of a weak gospel is always there. Much more thinking needs to be done about this, and in particular we need studies of how the rural church is actually to be a church in every sense.

9. Ecumenical

There is a substantial section on ecumenical activities (11.42ff) in the chapter of the report which covers mission. It raises several points about worship, referring readers back to the relevant section (9.26) in chapter 9.

One of these points concerns the non-Anglican at eucharistic worship. It is heartening to see the Commission's criticism (11.45) of the provisions of Canon B15A[1], describing it as having an 'inappropriate attitude' in the rural situation. Many rural parish churches do have non-Anglicans in their midst, either because people may not wish to travel some distance to a church of their own denomination, or because of a desire to worship in the local situation. Should such people move away from the village, then it cannot be assumed that they will worship in an Anglican church in future, and therefore it certainly is inappropriate to press anyone to be confirmed just to fulfil the tightest requirements of eucharistic discipline.

This section leads onto some remarks about Local Ecumenical Projects (11.45ff). The report recognizes the value of these and hopes that more will be developed. Unfortunately it does not address the causes of any inherited division between church and chapel, which may be sociological rather than religious. If such divisions are rooted in the social differences of previous centuries, then they may be hard to heal now. This is, of course, not impossible, provided that the real question is identified and handled with great senstivity and patience.

The report also mentions ecumenical activities (11.42) and also the inclusion of non-Anglicans in worship at the parish church (11.47). Lack of sensitivity can be a problem again here, especially since the Church of England is often so dominant in the countryside. Even the choice of the hymn tunes can make all the difference between making people feel welcome, and making them think that they are worshipping in an alien atmosphere.

This whole section is one of the most exciting parts of the report and firmly points the way ahead. It acknowledges (11.42) that local churches are often 'striding ahead of what is official policy'!

[1] This Canon requires that if non-Anglicans receive Holy Communion regularly in the parish church then they must consider being confirmed into the Church of England.

10. Multi-parish groups
The Commission clearly has thought carefully through the issue of whether there should be more joint services in a benefice. The arguments are only briefly rehearsed (9.25) but they highlight the major point, namely that it is desirable for there to be a service of worship in every community as often as possible. The advantages of the larger celebration are obvious but there will always be those who will not travel to another church. This last point is a slightly curious one. People may readily travel to a central point for everything else in their lives, but there still can be a great resistance to worshipping in another church. The report states this point and it would have been interesting to know if they had discovered any reasons for it.

There is no mention either of the effect that episcopal services have on the understanding of the local church, except for admitting that such services are normally held in the larger churches in an area (12.9). The Commission may have assumed that there is little alternative. A bishop recently suggested to me that perhaps bishops should visit as many of the churches as possible in a multi-parish group on a Sunday, confirming as they went! This is, after all, no different from what the rural clergy effectively do every Sunday of the year. It is a novel idea and could bring a great deal of encouragement to each of the local churches involved. However it will not be easy to achieve!

The difficulty with this sort of centralized activity, whether episcopal or parochial, is that it may focus on one particular church in a group, either because it is the largest or because it is where the incumbent lives or because it is in the largest village. This then creates a 'super-church' in the group and feelings of resentment may quickly follow.

11. The role of the deanery
The place of the deanery is only mentioned briefly (9.67) as a resource for the local church when looking at the music situation. There is a great deal more to be done at this level. If a deanery is focussed on a small town[1] then there may be scope for many deanery worship activities which will provide a resource for the local church as well as encouraging them to do more together.

12. Children and young people
The report stresses the need to encourage those who have young children to bring them to church and quotes the challenge of the General Synod report *Children in the Way* to recognize children as fellow pilgrims (9.45). It is interesting to see that 90% of those interviewed wanted children to come to worship in church alongside adults, but there is no indication of what that substantial group had in mind for such services. The reality is that often adults welcome children, provided the children conform to the adults' expectations. Instead it is better to indeed see the children as fellow members of the church and allow their expectations to be prominent as well.

[1] Preferably a *small* town because a large town can completely dominate the surrounding villages and their churches.

The report gives some helpful suggestions about incorporating the needs of children in church worship (9.47ff). Particularly important is the quotation from *Patterns for Worship* that 'actions speak louder than words.'[1] There are plenty of resource books around but they will need to be used carefully if we bear in mind the few children that are often present in rural churches. For example it is not easy to find an activity which satisfies three children who are part of a congregation of twelve when the children's ages are 3, 7 and 13.

Other parts of the report highlight the positive aspects of a local church school (10.25 and 10.35) and also the difficulties of keeping links with young people once they reach a certain age (10.74). There is surprisingly little about Sunday Schools.[2] Rural churches often lack facilities and this can be a very difficult problem to overcome if people want the Sunday School to meet at the same time as some of the church services. This problem is much related to the use of buildings, discussed below.[3]

13. Religious communities
The Commission draws our attention (9.18) to the need for support for the clergy through local lay groups and other resources from outside the parish. Is there perhaps a place for trying to build up religious communities again in the countryside, either by using existing large vicarages (and there are still a few around) or encouraging single people to use thir homes in this way? The beneficial effects of such groups cannot be overestimated.

14. Church organizations
The report is very positive about bellringing (9.69f) and also about the place in worship of village organizations (9.52). Something could be said too about the place of other groups such as the Mothers' Union, house groups etc, and not just about their general place in parish life but also how they can make specific contributions to worship by perhaps being responsible for a particular service or aspect of a service on a regular basis.

[1] See the report p.197. In point of fact diligent search (and an enquiry of Liturgical Commission members) has failed to locate this in an exact reference in *Patterns for Worship*! Even if it were a true quotation, it would remain as the only evidence (and that of most broad and general sort) of the ACORA team having actually looked at the Liturgical Commission's work in *Patterns*. One might have thought that, immediately *Patterns* was published, this rural Commission, having before them a chapter on worship to write, would have asked themselves what the implications of *Patterns* were for the countryside—even if they had then dismissed the Liturgical Commission's work as unhelpful. But no, they appear rather to have assumed that the Liturgical Commission was employed for the sake of urban parishes only. Was there *no* contact between the two over the last few years?.

[2] My making a statement like this is slightly dangerous because it is difficult to be sure of all the contents of such a long report, bearing in mind that this booklet is being written only a few weeks after publication of the report. What the statement really means is that I have not found much in the ACORA report about Sundays Schools which may not be quite the same thing!

[3] See Section 15 opposite.

15. Buildings

The section in the report on church buildings (mainly 11.12ff but also 9.41f) assumes that the Christian community will go on worshipping in the existing parish church. It is very positive about the reordering of such buildings and has some helpful pointers which may encourage those opposed to any change of this nature to see things in a very different light. But is the initial assumption right?

The parish church in a village does have an important place in rural life, and the effect of this must be understood by any seeking to minister in the countryside. It is important to keep these ancient buildings standing and using them to the full. It does not follow that it is necessarily the right place for the act of worship every Sunday. A cold church on a winter's Sunday morning is hardly inspiring and any benefits of the beauty of the building are quickly dispersed by unsuccessful efforts to keep warm. Surely good sense must prevail and perhaps on some occasions the church could meet elsewhere, such as in a hall or someone's house?

These sort of remarks will be heresy to some, but they are worth a PCC discussion, partly to get people to identify why they want to worship in the building. If, as a result, efforts are made to adapt the building to make it more 'user-friendly' then such a discussion will have been useful.

The reordering of buildings is often a very sensitive matter at parish level and all sorts of people can suddenly take a great deal of interest in what is happening. Patience, coupled with a certain amount of sensitive determination, is necessary for those seeking to make the changes!

In particular, buildings need to be considered in the light of what they are needed for rather than just as ancient monuments. The functional-versus-conservation discussion can become bitter and the report will help in providing material for further thought.

The previous chapter was deliberately presented as a series of questions to stimulate discussion. The report has provided much food for that discussion. The Commission have had a thankless task and are to be congratulated for providing some signposts for the future. Such a pilgrimage can only be for the good.

APPENDIX: THE RECOMMENDATIONS OF CHAPTER 9 OF THE REPORT

Some of the recommendations of this chapter have no immediate bearing on worship but are still reproduced here for the sake of completeness. The following is the full text:

1. Churches should establish some forum for discussion of work-related issues and parish clergy should make fuller use of industrial and agricultural chaplains (9.8).

2. PCCs should make provision for the costs of at least one retreat for their incumbent in their annual budget (9.17).

3. All clergy should give serious attention to their continuing study needs and make full use of the diocesan CME officer in assessing suitable courses (9.19).

4. Churchwardens and PCCs should ensure that clergy take the amount of holiday recommended by the diocese and that they are adequately financed to do so. Rural deans also need to help in ensuring that there is adquate clerical coverage for holidays (9.24).

5. Clergy should lead no more than two major services, in addition to an early said service, in any Sunday morning (9.24).

6. Each church should discuss the frequency of its communion services, reviewing its decision at intervals, in the light of the needs of the people it exists to serve (9.26).

7. Discussion on extended communion should be urgently reopened in the House of Bishops (9.30).

8. Those responsible for lay training in dioceses should give particular attention to the training needs of the laity involved in the planning and leading of worship and establish workshops and other resources to meet these needs (9.32 and 9.50).

9. Dioceses should establish and monitor pilot projects for lay leadership of worship in their parishes (9.37).

10. Each PCC should give serious consideration to the possibility of installing sound amplification including an induction loop in its church(es). Diocesan Advisory Committees should ensure that they can give guidance on this matter (9.42).

11. PCCs should be prepared to remunerate and pay all expenses of their regular musicians (9.66).

12. Cathedrals should review their resources and the potential that lies in these for supporting youth work, tourism, and parish worship, particularly in rural areas, for example by:
    (1) appointing a member of the chapter to have special responsibilities for the cathedral's involvement with youth work in the diocese;
    (2) using the cathedral's tourist facilities to signpost visitors to other churches in the diocese;
    (3) keeping in closer touch with parish clergy about what the cathedral can offer them in terms of resources (9.71-75).